Governing AI in Australia

Standards and Regulations

Dr Darryl J Carlton

Technics Publications

SEDONA, ARIZONA

115 Linda Vista, Sedona, AZ 86336 USA
https://www.TechnicsPub.com

Edited by Jamie Hoberman

Cover design by Lorena Molinari

First Printing 2024

Copyright © 2024 by Dr Darryl J Carlton

ISBN, print ed.	9781634625906
ISBN, Kindle ed.	9781634625913
ISBN, PDF ed.	9781634625920

Contents

Responsible AI: An Australian Perspective

Artificial Intelligence (AI) is rapidly reshaping the technological landscape of Australia, promising transformative benefits across various sectors of society and the economy. From healthcare and education to finance and public services, AI technologies are increasingly being deployed to enhance efficiency, drive innovation, and solve complex problems. The Australian government has recognised the potential of AI to boost productivity and improve the lives of citizens, estimating that the successful adoption of AI and automation could contribute between $170 billion to $600 billion to Australia's Gross Domestic Product (GDP) by 2030.

However, the swift advancement and widespread adoption of AI also bring significant challenges and risks that must be carefully managed. Issues such as algorithmic bias, privacy concerns, data security, and the potential for job displacement have raised important questions about the ethical and responsible development and deployment of AI systems. These concerns are not merely theoretical; they have real-world implications for individuals, communities, and the broader Australian society.

In response to these challenges, Australia has taken proactive steps to develop frameworks and guidelines for the responsible use of AI. The government has introduced several key initiatives, including Australia's AI Ethics Principles, the Voluntary AI Safety Standard, and the Policy for the responsible use of AI in government. These efforts reflect a growing recognition that robust governance mechanisms are essential to harness the benefits of AI while mitigating its potential risks.

This book argues that developing and implementing comprehensive, adaptive governance frameworks is crucial for Australia to fully realise the potential of AI technologies while safeguarding the rights, values, and interests of its citizens. By examining the current landscape of AI governance in Australia, identifying key principles for responsible AI development, and proposing practical steps for implementation, this book aims to contribute to the ongoing dialogue on how best to navigate the complexities of AI in the Australian context.

As AI continues to evolve at a rapid pace, so too must our approaches to governing it. This book will explore how Australia can position itself at the forefront of responsible AI innovation, balancing the need for technological advancement with the imperative to protect and promote the public good. By doing so, Australia has the opportunity not only to address the challenges posed by AI but also to set a global standard for ethical and effective AI governance.

The Promise and Perils of AI in the Australian Context

Potential Benefits of AI in Australia

Artificial Intelligence (AI) holds immense potential to transform various sectors of the Australian economy and society. Some key areas where AI is expected to make significant positive impacts include:

1. **Healthcare:** AI can enhance diagnostic accuracy, personalise treatment plans, and improve patient outcomes. For instance, the Commonwealth Scientific and Industrial Research Organisation (CSIRO) is developing AI-powered tools to detect and diagnose diseases earlier and more accurately.

2. **Agriculture:** In a country often challenged by harsh environmental conditions, AI can optimise crop yields, manage water resources more efficiently, and improve livestock management. The Australian government's National Agricultural Innovation Agenda includes AI as a key technology to boost agricultural productivity.

3. **Education:** AI-powered adaptive learning systems can personalise education, helping to address the diverse needs of students across Australia's vast geographic expanse.

4. **Public Services:** AI can streamline government services, making them more efficient and accessible. The Digital Transformation Agency is exploring AI applications to enhance service delivery and reduce administrative burdens.

5. **Environmental Management:** AI can help monitor and manage Australia's unique ecosystems, aiding conservation efforts and predicting and responding to natural disasters.

6. **Financial Services:** AI can enhance fraud detection, improve risk assessment, and provide personalised financial advice, potentially making financial services more secure and accessible to all Australians.

Key Risks and Challenges

While the potential benefits are significant, the deployment of AI in Australia also presents several risks and challenges that need careful consideration:

1. **Bias and Fairness:** There's a risk that AI systems may perpetuate or exacerbate existing biases, particularly against Indigenous Australians and other minority groups. Ensuring AI systems are fair and non-discriminatory is crucial in the diverse Australian context.

2. **Privacy Concerns:** With AI systems often requiring large amounts of data, there are concerns about how personal information is collected, used, and protected. This is particularly relevant given Australia's Privacy Act and its ongoing review process.

3. **Job Displacement:** While AI may create new job opportunities, it also has the potential to automate many existing roles. Australia needs to prepare for potential workforce disruptions and ensure a just transition.

4. **Security Risks:** As AI systems become more prevalent in critical infrastructure and government services, they may become targets for cyber attacks, posing national security risks.

5. **Transparency and Explainability:** Many AI systems, especially those based on deep learning, can be "black boxes," making it difficult to understand how they arrive at decisions. This lack of transparency can be problematic, especially in high-stakes domains like healthcare or criminal justice.

6. **Digital Divide:** There's a risk that the benefits of AI might be unevenly distributed, potentially exacerbating existing socio-economic disparities between urban and rural areas, or between different demographic groups.

7. **Ethical Concerns:** The use of AI in decision-making processes raises ethical questions about autonomy, accountability, and human oversight, particularly in sensitive areas like law enforcement or social services.

8. **Regulatory Challenges:** The rapid pace of AI development makes it challenging to create and maintain relevant regulations. Australia needs to develop flexible, adaptive regulatory frameworks that can keep pace with technological advancements.

Addressing these challenges while harnessing the benefits of AI will require a coordinated effort from government, industry, academia, and civil society. It necessitates the development of robust governance frameworks that can guide the responsible development and deployment of AI technologies in the unique Australian context.

Current Landscape of AI Governance in Australia

Australia has taken several significant steps towards establishing a framework for the responsible development and use of AI. This section outlines the key initiatives and documents that currently shape AI governance in Australia.

1. Australia's AI Ethics Principles

Developed by the Department of Industry, Science and Resources (DISR) in 2019, these principles provide a framework for ethical AI development and use:

1. Human, societal, and environmental wellbeing
2. Human-centred values
3. Fairness
4. Privacy protection and security
5. Reliability and safety
6. Transparency and explainability
7. Contestability
8. Accountability

These principles are voluntary but serve as a foundation for ethical AI practices across public and private sectors.

2. The Voluntary AI Safety Standard

Introduced in September 2024, this standard provides practical guidance to Australian organisations on how to safely and responsibly use and innovate with AI. Key features include:

- Ten voluntary guardrails apply to all organisations throughout the AI supply chain
- Focus on testing, transparency, and accountability requirements
- Guidance for both AI developers and deployers

3. Policy for the Responsible Use of AI in Government

Effective from September 2024, this policy aims to position the Australian Government as an exemplar in the safe and responsible use of AI. Key aspects include:

- Mandatory requirements for Non-corporate Commonwealth entities
- Designation of accountable officials for policy implementation
- Requirement for agencies to publish AI transparency statements
- Encouragement of staff training on AI fundamentals

4. Standard for Accountable Officials: Implementing Responsible AI Use in Australian Government

The Australian Government has introduced a Standard for Accountable Officials (AOs) to support the implementation of its Policy for Responsible Use of AI in Government. This standard outlines the responsibilities and best practices for designated officials who will oversee the adoption and management of AI within their respective agencies. The document provides crucial guidance on effectively implementing the policy, ensuring compliance, and fostering a culture of responsible AI use across the Australian Public Service (APS).

5. Standard for AI Transparency Statements: Enhancing Public Trust in Government AI Use

The Australian Government has introduced a Standard for AI Transparency Statements as part of its broader Policy for Responsible Use of AI in Government. This standard mandates that government agencies publish clear, consistent statements about their AI adoption and use. The initiative aims to build public trust, facilitate understanding, and enable comparison of AI use across government agencies.

6. National Framework for the Assurance of Artificial Intelligence in Government

This framework, developed jointly by Australian, state and territory governments, provides for a nationally consistent approach to AI assurance in government. It includes:

- Cornerstones of assurance: governance, data governance, risk-based approach, standards, and procurement
- Practical application of Australia's AI Ethics Principles in government contexts
- Guidance on implementing AI systems across various government functions

7. Privacy Act 1988: Regulates the handling of personal information by businesses and government agencies and establishes the thirteen (13) Australian Privacy Principles. The Privacy Act is about to get a complete makeover in the coming months.

8. Other Relevant Frameworks and Legislation

While not exclusively focused on AI, several other frameworks and laws play crucial roles in governing AI use:

- **Security of Critical Infrastructure Act 2018**: Imposes obligations relevant to AI systems in critical infrastructure. SOCI was expanded in 2024 to expand its oversight to eleven industrial sectors.
- **Consumer protection laws:** Relevant to AI applications in consumer-facing contexts
- **Human rights legislation:** Provides protections that must be considered in AI development and deployment

---

Gaps and Limitations in Current Approaches

While Australia has made significant progress in developing AI governance frameworks, several challenges remain:

1. **Voluntary Nature:** The current Australian guidelines are, for most organisations, voluntary, potentially limiting their effectiveness and consistent implementation.

2. **Rapid Technological Change:** The fast pace of AI development makes it challenging for governance frameworks to keep up.

3. **Implementation Challenges:** There's a need for more detailed guidance on how to implement the principles and standards in diverse contexts practically.

4. **Balancing Innovation and Regulation:** Finding the right balance between fostering innovation and ensuring adequate safeguards remains an ongoing challenge.

5. **Cross-Jurisdictional Issues:** As AI systems often operate across state and national boundaries, coordinating governance approaches can be complex.

As the AI landscape evolves, these governance frameworks must adapt and expand to address emerging challenges and opportunities.

ONE

The Australian Framework for AI Governance

The complex and far-reaching implications of AI necessitate a governance approach that involves multiple stakeholders across various sectors of Australian society. This section outlines a framework for AI governance that delineates the roles and responsibilities of key stakeholders while emphasising the need for collaboration and coordination.

Role of Government

The Australian government plays a central role in shaping the landscape of AI governance through legislation, regulation, and policy-making.

Federal Government

1. **Legislative Framework:** Develop and update laws to address AI-specific challenges, such as those related to privacy, data protection, and algorithmic decision-making.

2. **Regulatory Oversight:** Establish or empower regulatory bodies to monitor AI development and use, ensuring compliance with ethical principles and safety standards.

3. **National AI Strategy:** Continue to refine and implement a comprehensive national AI strategy that sets priorities, allocates resources, and coordinates efforts across different sectors.

4. **Public Sector AI Use:** Lead by example in the ethical and responsible use of AI in government services and operations, as outlined in the **"Policy for the responsible use of AI in government."**

5. **Research and Development Support:** Fund and promote AI research and development, focusing on beneficial AI that aligns with national interests and ethical principles.

State and Territory Governments

1. **Local Implementation:** Adapt and implement national AI strategies and frameworks to suit local contexts and needs.

2. **Sector-Specific Regulation:** Develop and enforce regulations for AI use in areas under state jurisdiction, such as healthcare and education.

3. **Public Awareness:** Conduct public education campaigns to increase AI literacy and awareness of AI's impacts at the community level.

Role of Industry

The private sector, as the primary developer and deployer of AI technologies, has a crucial role in ensuring responsible AI practices.

1. **Ethical AI Development:** Implement the **Voluntary AI Safety Standard** and adhere to Australia's **AI Ethics Principles** in developing and deploying AI systems.

2. **Self-Regulation:** Develop industry-specific best practices and standards for AI use, going beyond minimum regulatory requirements.

3. **Transparency:** Provide clear information about AI use in products and services, including potential limitations and risks.

4. **Collaboration:** Engage in public-private partnerships to address AI challenges and opportunities, sharing insights and best practices.

5. **Workforce Development:** Invest in AI education and training to build a skilled workforce capable of developing and managing AI responsibly.

Role of Civil Society

Non-governmental organisations, academia, and other civil society groups are vital in providing independent perspectives and advocacy.

1. **Research:** Conduct independent research on the societal impacts of AI, including ethical, legal, and social implications.

2. **Advocacy:** Represent public interests in AI governance discussions, advocating for responsible AI practices and policies.

3. **Education:** Contribute to public understanding of AI through educational programs and public engagement initiatives.

4. **Watchdog Function:** Monitor AI developments and their impacts, holding government and industry accountable for responsible AI practices.

Role of Academia

Academic institutions are crucial for advancing AI knowledge and fostering critical thinking about its implications.

1. **Fundamental Research:** Conduct cutting-edge research in AI technologies, algorithms, and their applications.

2. **Interdisciplinary Studies:** Promote interdisciplinary research on the ethical, legal, and social implications of AI.

3. **Education and Training:** Develop curricula and programs to train the next generation of AI professionals with a strong grounding in ethics and responsible practices.

4. **Policy Input:** Provide expert input to policymakers on AI-related issues, bridging the gap between technical knowledge and policy formulation.

Collaborative Mechanisms

To ensure effective AI governance, mechanisms for collaboration among these stakeholders are essential:

1. **Multi-Stakeholder Forums:** Establish regular forums for dialogue among government, industry, civil society, and academia on AI governance issues.

2. **Advisory Bodies:** Create AI advisory bodies with diverse representation to provide ongoing guidance on AI policy and regulation.

3. **Public Consultations:** Conduct wide-ranging public consultations on significant AI initiatives and policies.

4. **Information Sharing:** Develop platforms for sharing AI-related information, best practices, and lessons learned across sectors.

5. **Joint Research Initiatives:** Promote collaborative research projects involving multiple stakeholders to address complex AI challenges.

This multi-stakeholder framework recognises that effective AI governance in Australia requires the coordinated efforts of various sectors of society. By clearly defining roles while also emphasising collaboration, this approach aims to create a balanced and comprehensive governance ecosystem that can adapt to the rapidly evolving AI landscape while ensuring that AI development and deployment in Australia remains ethical, safe, and aligned with the public interest.

TWO

Australia's AI Ethics Principles

1. Human, Societal, and Environmental Wellbeing

This principle places the welfare of humans, society, and the environment at the forefront of AI development and deployment. It recognises that while AI has the potential to bring immense benefits, it must be developed and used responsibly to ensure these benefits are realised without causing unintended harm. This principle encourages developers and users of AI to consider the broader implications of their work beyond just the immediate application or business case.

For instance, an AI system designed to optimise urban traffic flow should not only consider efficiency in terms of travel times but also factor in environmental impacts such as emissions and noise pollution. Similarly, AI used in healthcare should aim to improve patient outcomes while considering broader societal impacts, such as equitable access to healthcare resources.

This principle also emphasises the importance of long-term thinking. AI developers and users are encouraged to consider how their systems might affect future generations and social structures. This could involve assessing the potential impact of AI on employment patterns, social interactions, or even cognitive development in the case of AI used in education.

Key points:

- AI should be used to improve quality of life and contribute to positive societal outcomes

- Environmental impacts of AI development and deployment should be considered and minimised
- Long-term effects on social structures and future generations should be taken into account

2. Human-Centred Values

The principle of Human-Centred Values ensures that AI systems are developed and deployed in a way that respects and upholds fundamental human rights and values. This principle is crucial in maintaining the ethical integrity of AI systems and ensuring they serve humanity rather than potentially undermining human agency or dignity.

In practice, this principle might manifest in various ways. For example, an AI system used in recruitment should be designed to promote diversity and equal opportunity rather than perpetuating existing biases. Similarly, AI used in social media content moderation should respect freedom of expression while protecting users from harm.

This principle also emphasises the importance of respecting cultural diversity. AI systems should be designed with an awareness of different cultural contexts and values, avoiding a one-size-fits-all approach that might inadvertently favour certain cultural perspectives over others.

Importantly, this principle underscores that AI should augment human decision-making rather than replace it entirely, especially in areas that require empathy, ethical judgment, or complex social understanding. For instance, while AI might assist in legal proceedings by processing vast amounts of data, critical decisions should ultimately be made by human judges who can consider nuanced ethical and social factors.

Key points:

- AI should not violate internationally recognised human rights
- Systems should respect and promote diversity
- Individual autonomy and the right to make decisions should be preserved

3. Fairness

The principle of Fairness in AI is fundamental to ensuring that the benefits of AI are distributed equitably and that AI systems do not exacerbate existing societal inequalities. This principle recognises that AI systems, if not carefully designed and implemented, have the potential to perpetuate or even amplify biases and discrimination.

Fairness in AI goes beyond just the absence of discrimination; it promotes inclusivity and accessibility. This means that AI systems should be designed to work effectively for all users, regardless of their characteristics or circumstances. For example, a voice recognition AI should be trained on diverse accents and languages to ensure it works equally well for all users.

Implementing fairness often requires proactive measures. This might involve carefully curating training data to ensure diverse representation, regularly auditing AI outputs for bias, and employing techniques like adversarial debiasing or fair representation learning.

It's important to note that fairness can be complex and context-dependent. What constitutes fair treatment may vary depending on the specific application and cultural context. Therefore, this principle also implies a need for ongoing dialogue and assessment to ensure AI systems meet fairness standards in their particular contexts of use.

Key points:

- AI should be designed to be inclusive and accessible to all, regardless of age, gender, ethnicity, or other characteristics
- Systems should be tested for bias and unfair outcomes
- Efforts should be made to ensure fair representation in data used to train AI systems

4. Privacy Protection and Security

In an era where data is often described as the new oil, the principle of Privacy Protection and Security is crucial in maintaining public trust in AI systems. This principle recognises that many AI systems rely on large amounts of data, often including personal information, and therefore must be developed and deployed with robust privacy protections and security measures.

Privacy protection in AI goes beyond just securing data; it involves respecting individuals' rights to control their personal information. This includes being transparent about what data is collected, how it's used, and allowing individuals to access, correct, or delete their data. For instance, an AI-powered smart home system should inform users about what data it collects and allow them to control or limit this collection.

Security, however, focuses on protecting AI systems and their data from unauthorised access, use, disclosure, disruption, modification, or destruction. This is particularly critical as AI systems are increasingly used in sensitive areas such as healthcare, finance, and critical infrastructure. A breach in an AI system could not only compromise personal data but could also lead to the system making incorrect or harmful decisions.

Implementing this principle often involves techniques such as data encryption, access controls, and regular security audits. It also requires staying up-to-date with evolving threats and best practices in cybersecurity. Furthermore, it involves considering privacy and security throughout the entire lifecycle of an AI system, from data collection and model training to deployment and ongoing operation.

Key points:

- AI should comply with privacy regulations and respect individuals' privacy rights
- Data used in AI systems should be protected from unauthorised access or breaches
- Security measures should be implemented to protect AI systems from attacks or misuse

5. Reliability and Safety

The principle of Reliability and Safety is crucial in ensuring that AI systems consistently perform as intended and do not cause harm. This principle recognises that as AI systems take on more critical roles in various domains, from healthcare to transportation, their reliability and safety become paramount.

Reliability in AI systems means consistently performing their intended functions under stated conditions over time. This requires rigorous testing and validation processes, not just before deployment but continuously throughout the system's lifecycle. For example, an AI system used for medical diagnosis should be consistently accurate across different patient populations and over time, even as it encounters new data.

Safety, however, focuses on ensuring that AI systems do not cause harm, either through their actions or failures. This involves anticipating potential risks and implementing safeguards. For instance, an autonomous vehicle must have multiple layers of safety systems to prevent accidents, even in unexpected situations.

Implementing this principle often involves formal verification, extensive testing in simulated environments, and gradual deployment with close monitoring. It also requires clear protocols for handling system failures or unexpected behaviours, including the ability to disable or override an AI system, if necessary, quickly.

Moreover, reliability and safety considerations should extend to the broader socio-technical system in which the AI operates. This includes considering how humans interact with the AI and ensuring that the overall system, not just the AI component, is reliable and safe.

Key points:

- AI systems should be thoroughly tested for reliability and safety before deployment
- Ongoing monitoring and evaluation should be conducted to ensure continued safe operation
- Mechanisms should be in place to handle failures or unexpected behaviours

6. Transparency and Explainability

The principle of Transparency and Explainability is fundamental to building trust in AI systems and ensuring their responsible use. This principle recognises that as AI systems increasingly impact essential aspects of people's lives, their operations and decision-making must be understandable and open to scrutiny.

Transparency in AI involves being open about when and how AI systems are being used, particularly when making or informing decisions that affect individuals or communities. This must involve, for example, clearly informing users when interacting with an AI chatbot rather than a human customer service representative or disclosing when AI has been used to personalise content or recommendations.

Explainability, often referred to as "interpretable AI" or "explainable AI" (XAI), goes a step further. It explains, in understandable terms, how an AI system arrived at a particular output or decision. This is particularly important for high-stakes decisions, such as those in healthcare, finance, or criminal justice. For instance, if an AI system recommends denying a loan application, the affected individual should be able to understand the key factors that led to this decision.

Implementing this principle can be challenging, particularly with complex AI systems like deep learning models, often described as "black boxes." However, various techniques are being developed to improve AI explainability, such as using simpler, more interpretable models where possible or employing techniques like LIME (Local

Interpretable Model-agnostic Explanations) or SHAP (SHapley Additive exPlanations) to provide insights into model decisions.

It's important to note that transparency and explainability should be balanced with other considerations, such as privacy and security. The level of detail provided should be appropriate to the context and the potential impact of the AI system.

Key points:

- Organisations should be transparent about their use of AI, especially in decisions that affect individuals
- AI decision-making processes should be explainable in understandable terms
- Information about the limitations and potential impacts of AI systems should be readily available

7. Contestability

The principle of Contestability ensures that individuals and groups can challenge the outcomes or use of AI systems that significantly impact them. This principle is crucial for maintaining accountability and fairness in AI deployments, particularly in high-stakes domains.

Contestability recognises that despite best efforts in design and testing, AI systems may sometimes produce errors or unfair outcomes. It provides a mechanism for affected parties to question and rectify these issues. For example, if an AI system is used in university admissions and a student believes they've been unfairly rejected, there should be a clear process to contest this decision and have it reviewed.

Implementing contestability involves several elements. First, there must be transparency about using AI and its role in decision-making processes. With this knowledge, individuals will know when or how to contest an AI-driven decision. Second, there should be clear, accessible processes for lodging and addressing contestations. This might involve having human reviewers who can examine contested decisions and override them if necessary.

Third, organisations using AI should be prepared to explain decisions in understandable terms, linking to the principle of explainability. Finally, there should be mechanisms for using the insights gained from contestations to improve the AI system, creating a feedback loop that enhances the system's fairness and accuracy over time.

It's worth noting that contestability doesn't mean that every AI decision must be subject to appeal, nor that human judgment should always override AI decisions. Rather, it ensures that safeguards are in place for significant decisions and that there's a way to identify and address systematic issues in AI systems.

Key points:

- Mechanisms should be in place for individuals to challenge AI-based decisions
- There should be clear processes for reviewing and addressing concerns about AI systems
- Human oversight should be available for significant AI-driven decisions

8. Accountability

The principle of Accountability ensures that there are clear lines of responsibility for the outcomes of AI systems throughout their lifecycle. This principle is crucial for maintaining trust in AI systems and ensuring they are developed and used responsibly.

AI's accountability extends beyond identifying who is responsible when things go wrong. It involves creating a culture and framework where all stakeholders - from developers and deployers to users and affected individuals - understand their roles and responsibilities in AI systems.

For developers, accountability might involve documenting design decisions, data sources, and testing procedures. For organisations deploying AI, it could mean conducting thorough impact assessments, implementing robust governance structures, and ensuring adequate human oversight.

Importantly, accountability also involves being answerable to external stakeholders. This could include regulatory compliance, but it goes beyond that to include broader societal accountability. For instance, companies using AI in ways that significantly impact the public might be expected to engage with community stakeholders and respond to their concerns.

Implementing accountability often involves creating clear governance structures, documentation processes, and audit trails. It may also include developing industry standards and best practices, as well as mechanisms for external auditing or certification of AI systems.

A key aspect of accountability is ensuring meaningful human oversight, particularly for high-impact AI systems. While AI can process information and make recommendations at a scale beyond human capability, humans should remain accountable for significant decisions and their outcomes.

Accountability also implies a commitment to continuous improvement. When issues are identified, there should be clear processes for addressing them and implementing lessons learned to improve future iterations of AI systems.

Key points:

- Clear lines of responsibility and accountability should be established for AI systems
- There should be mechanisms to assess compliance with these principles and relevant regulations
- Human oversight should be maintained, especially for high-impact AI systems

THREE

Australia's Voluntary AI Safety Standard: The Ten Guardrails

1. Establish, implement, and publish an accountability process including governance, internal capability, and a strategy for regulatory compliance.

This guardrail forms the foundation for an organisation's responsible use of AI. It emphasises the importance of creating transparent, documented processes for AI governance and accountability. This involves more than assigning responsibility; it requires developing a comprehensive strategy for managing AI across the organisation.

Organisations are expected to establish a transparent chain of command for AI-related decisions, ensuring that there are specific individuals or teams accountable for AI development, deployment, and monitoring. This accountability should be publicly disclosed, promoting transparency and trust.

Moreover, this guardrail underscores the need for building internal capability. This might involve training existing staff, hiring AI specialists, or partnering with external experts. The goal is to ensure that the organisation has the necessary expertise to make informed decisions about AI use and to manage associated risks effectively.

A key component of this guardrail is developing a strategy for regulatory compliance. As the AI landscape evolves, so too does the regulatory environment. Organisations need to stay abreast of these changes and have a clear plan for adapting to new requirements.

Key points:

- Assign clear accountability for AI governance within the organisation

- Develop and publish an AI strategy aligned with organisational goals
- Build internal AI capabilities through training and recruitment
- Create a plan for ongoing regulatory compliance

---

2. Establish and implement a risk management process to identify and mitigate risks.

This guardrail focuses on the critical need for proactive risk management in AI deployment. It recognises that while AI can offer significant benefits, it also introduces new and sometimes unforeseen risks that must be carefully managed.

Organisations are expected to develop a comprehensive risk management framework tailored explicitly to AI. This should include processes for identifying potential risks across various domains - technical, ethical, legal, and societal. Risk assessment should be an ongoing process, not a one-time event, as the risk landscape can change rapidly with evolving AI capabilities and applications.

Once risks are identified, organisations need to develop and implement mitigation strategies. This might involve technical solutions, such as improved testing protocols or fail-safe mechanisms, or procedural changes, like enhanced human oversight or stricter data governance.

Importantly, this guardrail emphasises that risk management should be proportionate to the potential impact of the AI system. High-stakes applications, such as AI used in healthcare diagnostics or financial decision-making, would require more rigorous risk management processes than lower-impact applications.

Key points:

- Develop a comprehensive AI risk management framework
- Conduct regular risk assessments throughout the AI lifecycle
- Implement appropriate risk mitigation strategies
- Ensure risk management efforts are proportionate to potential impact

3. Protect AI systems, and implement data governance measures to manage data quality and provenance.

This guardrail addresses the critical importance of data in AI systems. It recognises that the quality, security, and ethical use of data are fundamental to developing trustworthy and effective AI.

Organisations are expected to implement robust data governance frameworks. This includes measures to ensure data quality, such as processes for data cleaning, validation, and regular audits. Data provenance - understanding where data comes from and how it has been processed - is equally important. This helps ensure the reliability of AI outputs and can be crucial for explaining or auditing AI decisions.

Data protection is another key aspect of this guardrail. This involves not just cybersecurity measures to prevent unauthorised access or data breaches but also ethical considerations around data use. Organisations need to ensure they have appropriate consent for data use, especially when dealing with personal or sensitive information.

Moreover, this guardrail emphasises the need for ongoing data management throughout the AI lifecycle. As AI systems continue to learn and evolve, the data they use (and generate) needs to be continuously monitored and managed.

Key points:

- Implement robust data governance frameworks
- Ensure data quality through regular audits and validation processes
- Maintain clear records of data provenance
- Implement strong data protection measures, including cybersecurity and ethical use policies

4. Test AI models and systems to evaluate model performance and monitor the system once deployed.

This guardrail focuses on the crucial need for rigorous testing and ongoing monitoring of AI systems. It recognises that the performance and impacts of AI can change over time, especially as these systems are exposed to new data and scenarios in real-world deployment.

Organisations are expected to develop comprehensive testing protocols beyond technical performance metrics. Testing should also evaluate fairness, robustness, and alignment with intended use. This might involve techniques like adversarial testing, where systems are intentionally challenged with difficult or edge cases.

Importantly, this guardrail emphasises that testing and monitoring should continue after deployment. AI systems can drift over time, potentially leading to decreased performance or unexpected behaviours. Continuous monitoring allows organisations to detect these issues early and take corrective action.

This ongoing evaluation should also consider the broader impacts of the AI system. This might include monitoring for unintended consequences or assessing whether the system achieves its intended benefits in practice.

Key points:

- Develop comprehensive testing protocols that go beyond technical performance
- Conduct rigorous pre-deployment testing, including adversarial testing
- Implement systems for continuous monitoring post-deployment
- Regularly assess broader impacts and alignment with intended use

---

5. Enable human control or intervention in an AI system to achieve meaningful human oversight.

This guardrail underscores the importance of maintaining human control and oversight in AI systems. While AI can process information and make decisions at speeds and scales beyond human capability, this guardrail recognises that human judgment, ethical reasoning, and accountability remain crucial.

Organisations are expected to design AI systems with clear mechanisms for human intervention. This could range from "human-in-the-loop" systems, where AI assists human decision-makers, to "human-on-the-loop" systems, where humans monitor AI decisions and can intervene if necessary.

The level and nature of human oversight should be appropriate to the context and potential impact of the AI system. High-stakes or high-risk applications may require more direct and frequent human involvement, while lower-risk applications might need less intensive oversight.

Importantly, this guardrail also implies that organisations need to ensure that the humans providing oversight have the necessary skills, training, and authority to monitor and intervene in AI systems effectively. This might involve developing new roles or training programs focused on AI oversight.

Key points:

- Design AI systems with clear mechanisms for human intervention
- Ensure the level of human oversight is appropriate to the system's impact and risk
- Provide necessary training and authority for humans, providing oversight
- Maintain clear processes for human intervention in AI decision-making

6. Inform end-users regarding AI-enabled decisions, interactions with AI and AI-generated content.

This guardrail focuses on transparency and disclosure in AI use. It recognises that individuals have a right to know when interacting with or being impacted by AI systems, allowing them to make informed decisions and maintain agency in AI-mediated environments.

Organisations are expected to communicate when AI is used, particularly in customer-facing applications or when AI is involved in significant decisions. This could involve explicit labelling of AI-generated content, clear disclosures when interacting with AI chatbots or virtual assistants, or notifications when AI is used in decision-making processes.

Moreover, this guardrail encourages organisations to provide meaningful information about AI use. This goes beyond just disclosing the presence of AI to explaining (in accessible terms) what the AI is doing, what data it's using, and how it might impact the user.

This principle of informing users also extends to providing information about the limitations and potential biases of AI systems. Users should be aware of the contexts in which the AI's performance might be less reliable or where its decisions should be taken as suggestions rather than definitive answers.

Key points:

- Disclose when AI is being used, especially in customer-facing applications
- Provide meaningful explanations of how AI is being used and its potential impacts

- Label AI-generated content clearly
- Communicate the limitations and potential biases of AI systems to users

---

7. Establish processes for people impacted by AI systems to challenge use or outcomes.

This guardrail ensures that individuals have recourse when they believe an AI system has unfairly or negatively impacted them. It recognises that despite best efforts in design and deployment, AI systems may sometimes produce errors or unfair outcomes that must be addressed.

Organisations must establish clear, accessible processes for individuals to challenge AI-driven decisions or outcomes. This might involve setting up dedicated channels for AI-related complaints or appeals, ensuring that customer service staff are trained to handle AI-related inquiries, and having processes in place for human review of contested AI decisions.

Importantly, this guardrail also implies that organisations should be prepared to explain AI-driven decisions in understandable terms. This links back to transparency and explainability, ensuring that individuals have enough information to contest an outcome if they feel it's necessary meaningfully.

Organisations should view these challenges as opportunities for improvement. Feedback from these processes should be used to identify potential issues with AI systems and inform ongoing development and refinement.

Key points:

- Establish clear, accessible processes for challenging AI-driven decisions or outcomes
- Ensure staff are trained to handle AI-related inquiries and challenges
- Be prepared to provide explanations for AI-driven decisions
- Use feedback from challenges to improve AI systems

---

8. Be transparent with other organisations across the AI supply chain about data, models, and systems to help them effectively address risks.

This guardrail recognises the interconnected nature of AI development and deployment, often involving multiple organisations in a complex supply chain. It emphasises the importance of transparency and information sharing to ensure risks are effectively managed across the entire AI lifecycle.

Organisations must provide clear, detailed information about their AI systems, including the data used to train them, the models employed, and the system's capabilities and limitations. This information should be shared with other organisations in the supply chain, such as clients who will be deploying the AI or partners who are integrating the AI into larger systems.

This transparency allows each organisation in the chain to understand better and manage the risks associated with the AI system. For example, suppose your company is deploying an AI system developed by another firm. In that case, you need to understand the system's training data to assess potential biases or limitations and their applicability to your business and customers.

This guardrail encourages ongoing communication and collaboration across the AI supply chain. As new risks are identified or AI systems' performance evolves, this information should be shared to allow for coordinated risk management.

Key points:

- Provide detailed information about AI systems to others in the supply chain
- Share information about training data, models, and system capabilities/limitations
- Enable effective risk management across the entire AI lifecycle
- Maintain ongoing communication about evolving risks and performance issues

---

9. Keep and maintain records to allow third parties to assess compliance with guardrails.

This guardrail focuses on the importance of documentation and record-keeping in AI governance. It recognises that accountability and compliance can only be effectively assessed and demonstrated through clear, comprehensive records.

Organisations are expected to maintain detailed documentation throughout the AI lifecycle. This should include records of design decisions, data sources and processing, testing procedures and results, deployment processes, and ongoing monitoring and maintenance activities.

These records serve multiple purposes. They allow organisations to demonstrate compliance with these guardrails and other relevant regulations. They provide a basis for internal audits and continuous improvement. And they enable external audits or assessments, which may be required for certain high-impact AI applications.

Importantly, this guardrail implies that record-keeping should be an ongoing process, not a one-time event. As AI systems evolve and are updated, so too should the associated documentation. This creates a comprehensive audit trail that can be crucial for understanding the system's behaviour and decision-making over time.

Key points:

- Maintain detailed documentation throughout the AI lifecycle
- Include records of design decisions, data sources, testing, deployment, and monitoring
- Enable both internal and external audits of AI systems
- Ensure record-keeping is an ongoing process that evolves with the AI system

---

10. Engage your stakeholders and evaluate their needs and circumstances with a focus on safety, diversity, inclusion, and fairness.

This final guardrail emphasises the importance of stakeholder engagement in responsible AI development and deployment. It recognises that AI systems can have wide-ranging impacts on various groups and that understanding and addressing these impacts requires active engagement with affected stakeholders.

Organisations are expected to identify and engage with a diverse range of stakeholders throughout the AI lifecycle. This might include end-users, potentially affected communities, subject matter experts, and advocacy groups. The engagement should be meaningful and two-way, with organisations not just informing stakeholders about their AI plans but actively seeking input and feedback.

A key focus of this engagement should be on issues of safety, diversity, inclusion, and fairness. This involves assessing how the AI system might impact different groups, identifying potential biases or accessibility issues, and understanding diverse perspectives on what constitutes fair and beneficial AI use in other contexts.

This guardrail also implies an ongoing commitment to stakeholder engagement. As AI systems evolve and their impacts become clearer, organisations should continue to engage with stakeholders, reassess needs and circumstances, and adjust their approaches accordingly.

Key points:

- Identify and engage with a diverse range of stakeholders throughout the AI lifecycle
- Focus engagement on issues of safety, diversity, inclusion, and fairness
- Seek meaningful input and feedback, not just one-way communication
- Maintain ongoing stakeholder engagement as AI systems evolve

Policy for the Responsible Use of AI in Government

The Australian Government has introduced a new policy for the responsible use of AI in government, effective September 1, 2024. This policy aims to position the government as an exemplar in safe and responsible AI use, aligning with community expectations and complementing broader regulatory measures. The policy provides a unified approach for government agencies to confidently, safely, and responsibly engage with AI.

Key Findings

- The policy applies to all Non-corporate Commonwealth entities (NCEs) and encourages adoption by Corporate Commonwealth entities.

- It establishes a framework of mandatory requirements and recommended actions under three key principles: enable and prepare, engage responsibly, and evolve and integrate.

- The policy mandates the designation of accountable officials for AI implementation within 90 days of the policy taking effect.

- Agencies must publish an AI transparency statement within six months, detailing their approach to AI adoption and use.

- The policy emphasises the need for staff training, risk assessment, and ongoing monitoring and evaluation of AI use cases.

Recommendations

1. Designate accountable AI officials immediately to ensure compliance and coordinate AI initiatives.
2. Develop and publish comprehensive AI transparency statements to build public trust.
3. Implement AI fundamentals training for all staff within 6 months of the policy's effective date.
4. Establish internal AI use registers to track and manage AI deployments across the agency.
5. Participate in the pilot of the Australian Government's AI assurance framework to shape future governance practices.
6. Integrate AI considerations into existing frameworks for privacy, security, and data governance.

Mandatory Requirements

Accountable Officials

- Agencies must designate accountable official(s) within 90 days.
- Responsibilities include policy implementation, notifying the DTA of high-risk AI use cases, and engaging in whole-of-government AI coordination.

AI Transparency Statement

- Agencies must publish a statement outlining their AI approach within six months.
- The statement must be reviewed and updated annually or upon significant changes.
- It should include information on policy compliance, AI system monitoring, and public protection measures.

Impacts and Recommendations

Government Agencies

The introduction of the Policy for the Responsible Use of AI in Government represents a significant shift in how Australian government agencies approach artificial intelligence. This policy mandates a new level of accountability and transparency in AI use, which will have far-reaching implications for agency operations, decision-making processes, and public engagement strategies.

Government agencies now face the challenge of integrating AI governance into their existing organisational structures. This integration goes beyond mere compliance; it requires a fundamental rethinking of how agencies approach technology adoption and use. The policy's emphasis on transparency, through measures such as the mandatory AI transparency statement, will require agencies to develop new capabilities in AI ethics, risk assessment, and public communication.

To effectively navigate these changes, agencies should establish cross-functional AI governance teams. These teams should bring together expertise from IT, legal, policy, and communications departments to manage AI use's compliance and innovation aspects. The governance team's responsibilities should include overseeing the development and maintenance of the AI transparency statement, coordinating staff training initiatives, and liaising with the designated accountable officials.

Moreover, agencies should view this policy as an opportunity to become leaders in responsible AI use. By going beyond mere compliance and actively embracing the principles of ethical AI, agencies can enhance public trust, improve service delivery, and unlock new efficiencies in their operations. This proactive approach could involve developing agency-specific AI ethics guidelines, establishing regular AI audits, and actively engaging with citizens on AI-related issues.

IT Leaders

The new AI policy presents both challenges and opportunities for IT leaders within government agencies. The policy underscores the need for enhanced AI literacy across IT departments and the establishment of robust governance structures for AI systems.

IT leaders will be crucial in translating the policy's requirements into practical, implementable tech strategies.

The immediate impact on IT leaders will be the need to develop or enhance AI competency frameworks within their teams. This goes beyond technical skills; it includes fostering an understanding of AI ethics, risk assessment, and the societal implications of AI use. IT leaders should prioritise the development of training programs that cover not only the technical aspects of AI, but also its ethical and governance dimensions.

Another key area of focus for IT leaders should be integrating AI governance into existing IT processes. This includes updating change management procedures, security protocols, and data governance frameworks to accommodate AI-specific considerations. For instance, IT leaders might need to implement new monitoring tools to track AI system performance and detect potential biases or unintended consequences.

IT leaders should consider establishing dedicated AI centres of excellence within their departments to address these challenges. These centres can serve as hubs for AI expertise, providing guidance on AI project implementation, conducting internal audits, and staying abreast of evolving AI technologies and best practices. Additionally, IT leaders should foster close collaborations with other departments, particularly legal and policy teams, to ensure a holistic approach to AI governance.

IT leaders should position themselves as strategic partners in their agencies' AI initiatives. By proactively addressing AI adoption's technical and ethical challenges, IT leaders can help their agencies leverage AI to enhance public service delivery while maintaining public trust and policy compliance.

Procurement Officers

The Policy for the Responsible Use of AI in Government introduces new complexities into the procurement process for AI-related technologies and services. Procurement officers now face the challenge of incorporating AI-specific considerations into their evaluation criteria and contracting processes.

The impact on procurement practices will be substantial. Officers must now assess the technical capabilities and cost-effectiveness of AI solutions and their alignment with ethical AI principles, risk management frameworks, and transparency requirements. This expanded scope of evaluation requires procurement officers to develop new expertise in AI technologies and their potential impacts.

To address these new requirements, procurement officers should update their guidelines and evaluation criteria to include AI-specific considerations. This could involve developing a checklist of ethical AI principles that vendors must adhere to, or creating a scoring system that weighs factors such as algorithmic transparency, data privacy safeguards, and bias mitigation strategies.

Furthermore, procurement officers should work closely with IT and legal departments to develop standardised contract clauses for AI procurements. These clauses should address issues such as data ownership, algorithmic auditing rights, and vendor obligations for ongoing monitoring and reporting of AI system performance.

Another important consideration for procurement officers is the need to diversify their vendor pools to include specialists in Ethical AI and AI Governance. This may involve contacting academic institutions, think tanks, or specialised consultancies that can provide expertise in AI ethics and responsible AI development.

Procurement officers should also consider implementing a tiered approach to AI procurement, with more stringent requirements and oversight for high-risk AI applications. This could involve mandatory ethics reviews or independent audits for certain categories of AI systems.

By taking these steps, procurement officers can play a crucial role in ensuring that their agencies' AI adoptions align with the policy's requirements for responsible and ethical use. Their work will be instrumental in building an ecosystem of responsible AI vendors and setting industry standards for ethical AI development and deployment in the public sector.

Public Servants

The new AI policy has significant implications for public servants across all levels and departments of government. The policy's emphasis on AI literacy and responsible use means that understanding AI is no longer the sole purview of IT specialists; it's becoming an essential skill for the modern public servant.

The immediate impact on public servants will be the requirement to engage in AI training and awareness programs. This represents both a challenge and an opportunity for personal and professional development. Public servants must familiarise themselves with basic AI concepts, understand the ethical implications of AI use in government, and learn how to identify potential AI applications in their work.

To meet these new expectations, public servants should proactively engage with the AI training opportunities provided by their agencies. This engagement should go beyond passive participation; public servants should actively seek to apply their new knowledge to their specific roles and responsibilities. For instance, policy analysts might explore how AI could enhance their data analysis capabilities, while customer service representatives could investigate how AI chatbots might augment their work.

Moreover, public servants have a crucial role to play in identifying potential AI use cases within their departments. Their on-the-ground experience and domain expertise make them ideally placed to spot opportunities where AI could improve efficiency or service delivery. Agencies should establish clear channels for public servants to propose and discuss potential AI applications, fostering a culture of innovation and continuous improvement.

Public servants should also be encouraged to think critically about the ethical implications of AI use in their work. This could involve participating in ethical AI workshops, developing agency-specific AI guidelines, or serving on AI ethics committees. By actively engaging with these issues, public servants can help ensure that AI adoption in government aligns with public service values and ethical standards.

Furthermore, as the interface between government and citizens, public servants will play a key role in communicating about AI use to the public. They should be prepared to explain, in clear and accessible terms, how AI is being used in government services and what safeguards are in place to ensure responsible use.

By embracing these new responsibilities, public servants can position themselves as valuable contributors to their agencies' AI initiatives, enhancing their career prospects while helping to shape the future of AI in government.

Conclusion

The Australian Government's Policy for the Responsible Use of AI in Government marks a significant step towards ethical and transparent AI adoption in the public sector. By mandating accountability, transparency, and ongoing evaluation, the policy sets a framework for responsible AI use that balances innovation with public trust. Government agencies must act swiftly to meet the policy's requirements and leverage its recommendations to position themselves at the forefront of responsible AI adoption in public service delivery.

FIVE

Standard for Accountable Officials: Implementing Responsible AI Use in Australian Government

The Australian Government has introduced a Standard for Accountable Officials (AOs) to support the implementation of its Policy for Responsible Use of AI in Government. This standard outlines the responsibilities and best practices for designated officials who will oversee the adoption and management of AI within their respective agencies. The document provides crucial guidance on effectively implementing the policy, ensuring compliance, and fostering a culture of responsible AI use across the Australian Public Service (APS).

Key Components of the Standard

1. Designation of Accountable Officials

The standard requires agencies to designate Accountable Officials responsible for implementing the AI policy. Key points include:

- **Flexibility in selection:** AOs can be individuals or chairs of bodies, and responsibilities may be split across existing roles (e.g., CIO, CTO, CDO).

- **Cross-functional approach:** AOs may be selected from business or policy areas, not just technology departments.

- **Authority requirement:** Selected AOs should have sufficient influence to drive policy implementation effectively.

2. Core Responsibilities of Accountable Officials

AOs are tasked with several critical responsibilities:

- **Policy implementation:** Overseeing the agency's implementation of the AI policy.

- **Risk reporting:** Notifying the Digital Transformation Agency (DTA) of new high-risk AI use cases.

- **Coordination:** Serving as a contact point for whole-of-government AI coordination.

- **Engagement:** Participating in whole-of-government AI forums and processes.

- **Adaptability:** Staying updated on evolving requirements and policy changes.

3. Implementation Guidance

The standard provides detailed guidance on how AOs should approach policy implementation:

- **Holistic implementation:** Agencies should implement the entire policy as soon as practical, considering their context, size, and function.

- **Mandatory timelines:** Specific actions must be completed within stipulated timeframes.

- **Cultural shift:** AOs should embed a culture that balances AI risk management with innovation.

- **Cross-agency collaboration:** Facilitating involvement in government-wide coordination efforts.

4. Recommended Activities

The standard suggests several activities for AOs to consider:

- Developing a policy implementation plan

- Monitoring and measuring the implementation of each policy requirement

- Encouraging AI fundamentals training for all staff

- Promoting additional training for staff involved in AI procurement, development, and deployment

- Reviewing policy implementation regularly and providing feedback to the DTA

5. Transparency and Reporting

AOs play a crucial role in maintaining transparency:

- **Transparency statements:** AOs should provide the DTA with links to their agency's AI transparency statements.

- **High-risk use case reporting:** AOs must inform the DTA of any new or re-assessed high-risk AI use cases, including details on the type of AI, intended application, risk assessment rationale, and potential sensitivities.

6. Engagement and Coordination

The standard emphasises the importance of cross-government collaboration:

- **Forum participation:** AOs must engage in or delegate representatives to whole-of-government AI forums and processes.

- **Information sharing:** AOs should facilitate connections between their agency and the DTA for information collection and coordination activities.

Analysis and Implications

Flexibility and Adaptability

The standard's approach to designating AOs allows agencies to tailor implementation to their specific structures and needs. This flexibility is crucial given the diverse nature of government agencies and their varying levels of AI readiness. However, it also places a significant responsibility on agencies to select appropriate officials who can effectively drive AI governance.

Cultural Transformation

By making AOs responsible for embedding a culture of responsible AI use, the standard recognises that successful AI implementation goes beyond technical considerations. This cultural aspect is critical for long-term success and public trust but may present challenges in agencies with entrenched practices or limited AI exposure.

Risk Management Focus

The emphasis on reporting high-risk AI use cases reflects a proactive approach to risk management. This requirement allows for the development of government-wide risk mitigation strategies but may also raise concerns about potential constraints on innovation if not balanced carefully.

Cross-Government Coordination

The standard's focus on whole-of-government coordination through forums and information sharing is a strength. This approach can foster consistency in AI implementation across the APS and facilitate the sharing of best practices. However, the success of this coordination will depend on the active engagement of AOs and the effectiveness of the forums established.

Continuous Learning and Adaptation

The requirement for AOs to stay updated on policy changes acknowledges the rapidly evolving nature of AI technology and governance. This emphasis on continuous learning is crucial but may significantly burden AOs, particularly in smaller agencies with limited resources.

Recommendations for Effective Implementation

1. **Comprehensive Training Programs:** Agencies should develop robust AI training programs not only for general staff but also for specialised training for AOs to ensure they can effectively fulfil their responsibilities.

2. **Cross-Agency Collaboration Networks:** Establish formal networks for AOs across agencies to share experiences, challenges, and best practices in AI policy implementation.

3. **AI Governance Frameworks:** Develop agency-specific AI governance frameworks that align with the national policy but address unique agency contexts and risks.

4. **Regular Policy Review Mechanisms:** Implement systematic review processes to assess the effectiveness of AI policy implementation and identify areas for improvement.

5. **Public Engagement Strategies:** Develop strategies for AOs to engage with the public on AI initiatives, enhancing transparency and building trust in government AI use.

Conclusion

The Standard for Accountable Officials represents a significant step towards ensuring responsible AI use across the Australian Government. Clearly defining the roles and responsibilities of AOs, it provides a framework for consistent and ethical AI implementation. However, the success of this standard will largely depend on how effectively agencies can select and support their AOs, and how well AOs can navigate the complex landscape of AI governance.

As AI technology evolves rapidly, this standard and the broader AI policy will likely require regular updates. The standard's flexibility should allow for such adaptations, but it will be crucial for the DTA and AOs to maintain open lines of communication and remain agile in their approach to AI governance.

Implementing this standard has the potential to position Australia as a leader in responsible government AI use, but to fully realise this potential, it will require ongoing commitment, resources, and collaboration across all levels of government.

Six

Standard for AI Transparency Statements: Enhancing Public Trust in Government AI Use

The Australian Government has introduced a Standard for AI Transparency Statements as part of its broader Policy for Responsible Use of AI in Government. This standard mandates that government agencies publish clear, consistent statements about their AI adoption and use. The initiative aims to build public trust, facilitate understanding, and enable comparison of AI use across government agencies. This report analyses the key components of the standard and its implications and provides recommendations for effective implementation.

Key Components of the Standard

1. Mandatory Disclosure Requirements

Agencies must provide specific information in their transparency statements:

- Intentions behind AI use or consideration
- Classification of AI use (usage patterns and domains)
- Identification of direct public interaction with AI systems
- Measures for monitoring AI system effectiveness
- Compliance with relevant legislation and regulations
- Efforts to protect the public from negative impacts
- Compliance with the Policy for Responsible Use of AI in Government
- Date of the most recent update

2. Publication and Accessibility

- Statements must be published on the agency's public-facing website
- Recommended placement in a global menu, similar to privacy policies
- Use of clear, plain language consistent with the Australian Government Style Manual

3. Regular Review and Updates

Agencies must review and update their statements:

- At least annually
- When making significant changes to their AI approach
- When new factors materially impact the statement's accuracy

4. AI Classification System

The standard provides a classification system for AI use, including:

- Usage patterns (e.g., decision making, analytics, workplace productivity)
- Domains (e.g., service delivery, compliance, law enforcement)

Analysis and Implications

1. Promoting Transparency and Trust

The standard's primary goal is to enhance public trust in government AI use through transparency. By mandating clear, accessible information about AI adoption and management, it addresses growing public concerns about AI's impact on government services and decision-making. This approach aligns with global trends in AI governance and could position Australia as a leader in transparent government AI use.

2. Standardisation and Comparability

The prescribed format and content requirements create a standardised approach across agencies. This uniformity will likely facilitate easier comparison of AI use across different government bodies, potentially driving consistency and best practices in AI adoption. However, it may also highlight discrepancies in AI readiness and implementation across agencies.

3. Balancing Disclosure and Security

While the standard promotes transparency, it also allows agencies to provide high-level overviews rather than detailed use cases. This balance is crucial, especially for agencies dealing with sensitive information or national security. However, it may lead to challenges in determining the appropriate level of detail to disclose without compromising operational security or competitive advantage in AI development.

4. Adaptation to Rapid AI Evolution

The requirement for regular updates acknowledges the fast-paced nature of AI development. This adaptability is crucial but may pose challenges for agencies in terms of resource allocation and the need for continuous monitoring of AI deployments and policy changes.

5. Public Engagement and Accountability

The standard facilitates public engagement on AI issues by providing a public contact email and using plain language. This openness could lead to increased public scrutiny and drive more responsible AI use. However, it may also increase the workload for agencies in managing public inquiries and concerns.

6. Classification System Impact

The provided classification system for AI use offers a structured way to categorise AI applications. This could aid in identifying trends, gaps, and potential areas of concern across government AI use. However, as AI capabilities expand, this classification system may need regular updates to remain relevant.

Recommendations

1. **Develop Robust Internal Processes:** Agencies should establish comprehensive internal processes for AI inventory, classification, and regular review to ensure accurate and timely updates to transparency statements.
2. **Invest in AI Literacy:** Enhance AI literacy across agency staff to ensure accurate classification and description of AI systems in transparency statements.
3. **Establish Cross-Agency Collaboration:** Create forums for agencies to share best practices in crafting transparency statements and addressing public inquiries.
4. **Implement Monitoring Tools:** Invest in AI monitoring and auditing tools to effectively track AI system performance and impacts, supporting the required reporting on effectiveness and public protection measures.
5. **Engage with Stakeholders:** Regularly engage with both the public and AI experts to gather feedback on the clarity and usefulness of transparency statements.
6. **Prepare for Scalability:** Design processes and systems that can scale as AI use in government expands, ensuring the ability to maintain comprehensive and accurate transparency statements over time.

Conclusion

The Standard for AI Transparency Statements represents a significant step towards open and responsible AI use in the Australian Government. Mandating clear, consistent public disclosure of AI adoption and management practices can enhance public trust and drive more thoughtful AI implementation across agencies.

However, the success of this initiative will depend on how effectively agencies can implement these requirements while balancing operational needs and security considerations. As AI technology and its applications continue to evolve rapidly, the standard and its implementation will likely require ongoing refinement.

This transparency initiative positions Australia as a potential global leader in responsible government AI use. Its impact may extend beyond the public sector, influencing AI governance practices in the private sector and shaping public expectations for AI transparency across all domains.

SEVEN

National Framework for AI Assurance in Australian Government: A Strategic Analysis

The Australian, state, and territory governments have jointly developed a National Framework for the Assurance of Artificial Intelligence in Government. This framework, released on June 21, 2024, establishes a coordinated approach to ensure the safe and responsible use of AI across all levels of government in Australia. It aligns with Australia's AI Ethics Principles and broader initiatives on safe and responsible AI use.

Key Findings

1. **Unified Approach:** The framework creates a nationally consistent methodology for AI assurance, providing clarity and certainty for government agencies and their partners.

2. **Ethics-Driven:** Built on Australia's AI Ethics Principles, the framework emphasises human-centric, ethical AI use in government.

3. **Flexibility and Adaptability:** The framework acknowledges the rapidly evolving nature of AI and is designed to be flexible and responsive to technological advancements.

4. **Risk-Based Implementation:** It advocates for a risk-based approach, allowing for streamlined processes in low-risk scenarios while ensuring rigorous oversight for high-risk AI applications.

5. **Comprehensive Coverage:** The framework addresses key areas, including governance, data management, procurement, and transparency.

Strategic Implications

For Government Agencies

1. **Enhanced Accountability:** Agencies will need to establish clear roles and responsibilities for AI oversight, potentially requiring organisational restructuring.

2. **Skill Development:** There will be an increased need for AI literacy across all levels of government, necessitating significant investment in training and education.

3. **Procurement Challenges:** Agencies may face new complexities in AI-related procurement, requiring updates to existing processes and evaluation criteria.

For Technology Vendors

1. **Market Opportunity:** The framework's implementation will likely drive demand for AI governance tools, explainable AI solutions, and AI assurance services.

2. **Compliance Requirements:** Vendors serving government clients will need to align their offerings with the framework's principles and requirements.

3. **Transparency Expectations:** There will be increased pressure on vendors to provide more transparent and explainable AI solutions.

For Citizens

1. **Increased Trust:** The framework aims to build public confidence in government AI use through enhanced transparency and ethical standards.

2. **Rights Protection:** Citizens can expect stronger protections and clearer mechanisms for contesting AI-influenced decisions.

3. **Service Improvements:** The responsible adoption of AI in government could lead to more efficient and personalised public services.

Key Components of the Framework

1. Cornerstones of Assurance

- AI & Project Governance
- Data Governance
- Risk-based approach
- Standards alignment
- Procurement considerations

2. Implementation of AI Ethics Principles

- Human, societal, and environmental wellbeing
- Human-centered values
- Fairness
- Privacy protection and security
- Reliability and safety
- Transparency and explainability
- Contestability
- Accountability

3. Practical Guidelines

The framework provides specific practices for each ethical principle, offering practical guidance for implementation.

Challenges and Risks

1. **Implementation Complexity:** The comprehensive nature of the framework may pose challenges for smaller agencies with limited resources.

2. **Balancing Innovation and Regulation:** There's a risk that overly cautious interpretation of the framework could stifle AI innovation in government.

3. **Skill Gap:** The current shortage of AI expertise in the public sector may hinder effective implementation.

4. **Technological Pace:** The rapid evolution of AI technology may outpace the framework's ability to adapt, requiring frequent updates.

5. **Interoperability:** Ensuring consistent application across different levels of government and jurisdictions could be challenging.

Recommendations

1. **Phased Implementation:** Government agencies should adopt a staged approach, focusing first on high-risk AI applications and gradually expanding to cover all AI use cases.

2. **Cross-Agency Collaboration:** Establish forums for sharing best practices and lessons learned to accelerate the learning curve across government.

3. **Public-Private Partnerships:** Engage with the private sector to leverage expertise in AI governance and assurance.

4. **Continuous Education:** Invest in ongoing AI literacy programs for public servants at all levels.

5. **Regular Framework Reviews:** Establish a process for annual reviews and updates to the framework to ensure it remains relevant as AI technology evolves.

6. **Transparency Initiatives:** Develop public-facing dashboards or reports to showcase progress in implementing the framework and building trust.

7. **International Engagement:** Actively participate in global AI governance initiatives to share learnings and align with international best practices.

Conclusion

The National Framework for the Assurance of AI in Government represents a significant step towards responsible AI use in the Australian public sector. Its comprehensive and principle-based approach positions Australia as a potential leader in government AI governance. However, the success of this initiative will depend on effective implementation, ongoing adaptation, and a balance between ethical considerations and innovation. As AI continues to evolve rapidly, this framework will likely require regular updates to remain relevant and effective.

EIGHT

Australian Privacy Principles

The Australian Privacy Principles, part of the Privacy Act 1988 (Cth), regulate the handling of personal information by federal government agencies and private organisations with an annual turnover exceeding AUD$3 million. These principles form the cornerstone of privacy protection in Australia.

Please keep in mind that as of November 2024, changes to the privacy legislation have been referred to the Senate for review. I shall discuss the proposed changes at the end of this chapter.

Principle 1: Open and Transparent Management of Personal Information

This principle sets the foundation for transparency in an organisation's handling of personal information. It emphasises the importance of clear communication with individuals about how their data is managed. By requiring organisations to develop and maintain a comprehensive privacy policy, **APP 1** ensures that individuals can easily understand what information is being collected about them, why it's being collected, and how it will be used and protected. This transparency builds trust and empowers individuals to make informed decisions about sharing their personal information.

- Develop and maintain a clear, up-to-date privacy policy

- Implement practices, procedures, and systems to ensure APP compliance

- Make the privacy policy freely available and easily accessible

- Include in the policy types of information collected, purposes of collection, complaint processes, and potential overseas disclosures

Principle 2: Anonymity and Pseudonymity

APP 2 recognises the importance of individual privacy by giving people the option to interact with organisations without fully revealing their identity. This principle acknowledges that in many situations, an organisation doesn't need to know exactly who they're dealing with to provide a service or conduct business. By allowing anonymity or the use of pseudonyms, it protects individual privacy and gives people more control over their personal information. However, it also recognises that there are times when identification is necessary or required by law.

- Allow individuals to remain anonymous or use a pseudonym when dealing with the organisation

- Exceptions apply when impractical or when required by law to identify individuals

Principle 3: Collection of Solicited Personal Information

This principle governs how organisations can collect personal information. It emphasises the need for restraint and relevance in data collection, ensuring that organisations only gather information that's truly necessary for their functions or activities. By requiring that information be collected lawfully and fairly, preferably directly from the individual, it promotes transparency and consent in data gathering. The principle also recognises that some types of information, such as sensitive data, require more protection and explicit consent for collection.

- Only collect personal information that is reasonably necessary for the organisation's functions or activities

- Collect information by lawful and fair means, preferably directly from the individual

- Obtain consent when collecting sensitive information, with some exceptions

Principle 4: Dealing with Unsolicited Personal Information

APP 4 addresses the common situation where organisations receive personal information they didn't ask for or actively collect. This might happen through misdirected communications, excess information provided by individuals, or data received from third parties. The principle requires organisations to consciously decide whether they could have collected this information lawfully if they had solicited it. If they do, they must responsibly dispose of or de-identify the information, ensuring that they don't retain or use personal data they shouldn't have.

- Determine if unsolicited information could have been collected under **APP 3**

- If not collectible under **APP 3**, destroy or de-identify the information as soon as practicable

- If retained, ensure compliance with other APPs

Principle 5: Notification of the Collection of Personal Information

Transparency is at the heart of **APP 5**. This principle ensures that individuals are fully informed about the collection of their personal information at or around the time it's collected. By requiring organisations to provide detailed information about who is collecting the data, why it's being collected, and how it will be used and shared, **APP 5** empowers individuals to make informed decisions about their personal information. It also helps build trust between organisations and the individuals they interact with.

- Notify individuals about the collection of their personal information at or before the time of collection, or as soon as practicable afterwards

- Provide details about the organisation's identity and contact details, purposes of collection, consequences of non-collection, disclosure practices, and access/correction rights

Principle 6: Use or Disclosure of Personal Information

APP 6 sets clear boundaries on how organisations can use or share the personal information they've collected. It establishes the *'primary purpose'* of collection and ensures that information is generally only used for this purpose. However, it also recognises legitimate reasons why information might need to be used or disclosed for other purposes. Allowing secondary use or disclosure under specific conditions, such as with consent or for closely related purposes, balances the protection of individual privacy with practical business needs and public interest considerations.

- Use or disclose personal information only for the primary purpose of collection.

- Secondary use or disclosure is allowed with consent or under specific exceptions, such as related purposes within reasonable expectations, legal requirements, or public interest scenarios.

Principle 7: Direct Marketing

This principle explicitly addresses the use of personal information for direct marketing, a practice that can be particularly intrusive if not properly managed. **APP 7** generally prohibits using personal information for direct marketing unless specific conditions are met. Requiring organisations to obtain consent or establish a reasonable expectation for marketing communications and mandating easy opt-out mechanisms gives individuals control over how their information is used for marketing purposes. This principle strikes a balance between legitimate business interests and individual privacy rights.

- Generally prohibit the use of personal information for direct marketing

- Allow exceptions when the individual would reasonably expect it, and an easy opt-out is provided

- Require consent for sensitive information use in direct marketing

- Always include a prominent opt-out option in marketing communications

Principle 8: Cross-border Disclosure of Personal Information

In an increasingly globalised world, **APP 8** addresses the crucial issue of personal information being sent overseas. It recognises that once information leaves Australia, it may no longer be protected by Australian privacy laws. Therefore, this principle places responsibility on the Australian organisation to ensure that overseas recipients handle the information to the same standard as the Australian Privacy Principles. By making the disclosing entity accountable for breaches by overseas recipients, it encourages due diligence in international data transfers and maintains protection for personal information, regardless of its geographical location.

- Before disclosing personal information overseas, take reasonable steps to ensure the recipient doesn't breach the APPs

- The disclosing entity may be accountable for overseas recipients' breaches

- Exceptions include consent after being expressly informed, or legally authorised disclosures

Principle 9: Adoption, Use, or Disclosure of Government-Related Identifiers

APP 9 recognises the special status of government-related identifiers, such as tax file numbers or driver's license numbers. These identifiers are designed for specific government purposes. Their widespread use by other organisations could lead to privacy risks, including increased potential for identity theft or unauthorised linking of personal information across different contexts. By restricting the adoption, use, or disclosure of these identifiers, this principle helps maintain the separation between government and private sector information handling, protecting individual privacy and limiting the expansion of any single identifier into a de facto national identity number.

- Restrict the adoption, use, or disclosure of government-related identifiers (e.g., Medicare numbers)

- Exceptions include when required by law, for identity verification purposes, or when prescribed by regulations.

Principle 10: Quality of Personal Information

This principle underscores the importance of maintaining accurate, up-to-date, and complete personal information. Only accurate or updated information can lead to fair outcomes for individuals, whether in terms of service delivery, decision-making, or representation of the individual. **APP 10** obligates organisations to take reasonable steps to ensure the quality of the personal information they hold. This protects individuals from potential harm caused by poor-quality data and enhances the value and utility of the information for the organisation itself.

- Take reasonable steps to ensure personal information is accurate, up-to-date, and complete.

- Ensure information is relevant to the purpose of use or disclosure.

Principle 11: Security of Personal Information

APP 11 addresses the critical issue of information security in an age of increasingly common data breaches and cyber threats. It requires organisations to proactively protect personal information from various risks, including unauthorised access, modification, disclosure, and loss. This principle also recognises that holding onto personal information indefinitely increases security risks. By requiring the destruction or de-identification of information that's no longer needed, **APP 11** minimises the potential impact of data breaches. It respects the temporal nature of the original reasons for data collection.

- Take reasonable steps to protect personal information from misuse, interference, loss, unauthorised access, modification, or disclosure.

- Destroy or de-identify information that is no longer needed unless required by law to retain it.

Principle 12: Access to Personal Information

This principle embodies the fundamental right of individuals to know what information an organisation holds about them. By providing individuals with access to their personal information upon request, **APP 12** promotes transparency and accountability in information handling practices. It empowers individuals to verify the accuracy of their information and understand how it's being used. However, the principle also recognises that there are situations where access might not be appropriate, such as when it would impact the privacy of others or interfere with legal proceedings. In these cases, organisations must provide reasons for refusing access.

- Provide individuals access to their personal information upon request.

- Respond to access requests within a reasonable period.

- Provide written reasons if access is refused, based on specific grounds (e.g., legal proceedings, commercial sensitivities).

Principle 13: Correction of Personal Information

APP 13 complements the access rights provided in APP 12 by allowing individuals to correct their personal information when it's inaccurate, out-of-date, incomplete, irrelevant, or misleading. This principle recognises that personal circumstances change and that errors can occur in data collection or management. By requiring organisations to correct information and notify other entities if that information has been shared, it helps maintain the overall quality and accuracy of personal information in circulation.

This principle is crucial for ensuring fair treatment of individuals based on their personal information.

- Take reasonable steps to correct personal information to ensure it is accurate, up-to-date, complete, relevant, and not misleading.

- Notify other entities of corrections if previously shared.

- Provide reasons for refusal to correct and options for recourse.

These principles collectively form a comprehensive framework for the responsible handling of personal information by organisations in Australia. They balance the need for organisations to collect and use personal information with the right of individuals to privacy and control over their data. Compliance with these principles is not just a legal requirement but a fundamental aspect of building trust with customers and maintaining ethical business practices in the digital age.

NINE

Proposed Changes to the Australian Privacy Act

Australia is undertaking a significant overhaul of its privacy laws, as the government responds to the comprehensive Privacy Act Review Report. This initiative aims to bridge the gap between Australia's current privacy standards and the global benchmark set by the European Union's General Data Protection Regulation (GDPR). The proposed reforms come at a crucial time, with recent surveys indicating growing concern among Australians about the safety of their personal data in the digital age.

The government has committed to implementing a range of changes that will reshape the privacy landscape in Australia. These include strengthening security measures for personal information, introducing new regulations for automated decision-making, enhancing children's privacy online, and revamping enforcement mechanisms with tiered civil penalties and expanded powers for the Information Commissioner.

Key areas of focus include reevaluating exemptions for small businesses and employee records, refining the journalism exemption, and aligning the Notifiable Data Breaches scheme more closely with international standards. The reforms also propose introducing concepts like 'controllers' and 'processors' to clarify responsibilities in data handling.

These changes reflect a delicate balance between fostering digital innovation and safeguarding individual privacy rights. By updating its privacy framework, Australia aims to not only protect its citizens more effectively but also maintain its competitive edge in the global digital economy.

The changes which have made their way into the proposed legislation are:

1. Objects of the Act

The bill aims to strengthen the emphasis on protecting privacy and recognising the public interest in privacy protection.

2. APP Codes

It gives the Minister and Commissioner more power to develop and implement Australian Privacy Principle (APP) codes, including temporary codes for urgent situations.

3. Emergency Declarations

The bill revises the process for making emergency declarations related to privacy, clarifying what information can be shared and for what purposes during emergencies.

4. Children's Privacy

A new Children's Online Privacy Code will be developed to enhance privacy protections for children online.

5. Security and Data Retention

The bill emphasises the need for technical and organisational measures to protect personal information.

6. Overseas Data Flows

It introduces stricter requirements for sharing personal information with overseas recipients.

7. Data Breach Notifications

The bill establishes a framework for responding to eligible data breaches, including allowing the Minister to make declarations to prevent or reduce harm from breaches.

8. Penalties

It increases penalties for serious privacy breaches and introduces a tiered penalty system.

9. Court Powers

Courts will have expanded powers to make orders in privacy breach cases, including awarding damages and requiring corrective actions.

10. Public Inquiries

The Commissioner will have the power to conduct public inquiries into privacy matters.

11. Automated Decisions

Organisations using automated decision-making systems that significantly affect individuals must disclose this in their privacy policies.

12. Serious Invasions of Privacy

The bill introduces a new statutory tort for serious invasions of privacy, allowing individuals to sue for privacy breaches in certain circumstances.

13. Doxxing Offenses

New criminal offences are introduced for "doxxing" - maliciously sharing someone's personal information online.

These changes aim to modernise Australia's privacy laws, increase protections for individuals (especially children), and provide stronger enforcement mechanisms for privacy breaches.

TEN

AI Governance: A Standards Perspective

This report analyses the AS ISO/IEC 42001:2023 standard, which specifies requirements for establishing, implementing, maintaining, and continually improving an Artificial Intelligence Management System (AIMS) within an organisation. The standard is designed for entities providing or utilising AI-based products or services, ensuring responsible development and use of AI systems.

Key findings include

- The standard provides a comprehensive framework for organisations to manage AI-related risks and opportunities effectively.

- It emphasises the importance of leadership commitment, risk assessment, and continuous improvement in AI management.

- The standard applies to organisations of all sizes and types that provide or use AI systems.

- It aligns with other ISO management system standards, facilitating integration with existing organisational processes.

- The standard includes annexes with reference controls and implementation guidance for AI management.

Analysis

1. Scope and Applicability

The AS ISO/IEC 42001:2023 standard is designed to be universally applicable to any organisation that provides or uses products or services utilising AI systems, regardless of size, type, or nature. This broad applicability ensures that the standard can be adopted by a wide range of entities, from small startups to large multinational corporations, across various industries and sectors.

The standard's scope encompasses the entire lifecycle of AI systems, from development to deployment and use. It provides a structured approach for organisations to establish, implement, maintain, and continually improve their AI management system. This comprehensive coverage allows organisations to systematically address AI-related challenges and opportunities, ensuring responsible and effective use of AI technologies.

2. Context of the Organisation

The standard emphasises the importance of understanding the organisation's context when implementing an AI management system. This includes:

- Determining external and internal issues relevant to the organisation's purpose and ability to achieve the AI management system's intended results.

- It is particularly important to consider climate change, which is a potentially significant issue, as many experts are forecasting massive energy requirements for AI processing.

- Understanding the intended purpose of the organisation's AI systems developed, provided, or used.

- Identifying interested parties relevant to the AI management system and their requirements.

- Determining the scope of the AI management system, considering internal and external factors.

This contextual analysis ensures that the AI management system is tailored to the organisation's needs and circumstances, increasing its effectiveness and relevance.

3. Leadership and Commitment

The standard places significant emphasis on leadership involvement in the AI management system. Top management is required to demonstrate leadership and commitment by:

- Ensuring the establishment of AI ethics, policy, and objectives are aligned with the organisation's strategic direction.

- Integrating AI management system requirements into business processes.

- Providing necessary resources for the AI management system.

- Communicating the importance of effective AI management.

- Promoting continual improvement.

This focus on leadership ensures that AI management is given appropriate priority and resources within the organisation, fostering a culture of responsible AI use and development.

4. AI Policy

The standard requires organisations to establish an AI policy that:

- Is appropriate to the organisation's purpose.

- Provides a framework for setting AI objectives.

- Includes commitments to meet applicable requirements and continual improvement.

The AI policy is a guiding document for the organisation's approach to AI management, ensuring alignment with overall organisational goals and values.

5. Planning

The planning section of the standard covers several crucial aspects:

a)   **Actions to Address Risks and Opportunities:**

- Organisations must establish processes for AI risk assessment and treatment.

- The risk assessment process should be aligned with AI policy and objectives and produce consistent, valid, and comparable results.

- Risk treatment involves selecting appropriate options, determining necessary controls, and producing a statement of applicability.

b)   **AI System Impact Assessment:**

- Organisations must define a process for assessing the potential consequences of AI systems on individuals, groups, and societies (an ethics policy).

- The impact assessment should consider specific technical and societal contexts where AI systems are deployed.

c)   **AI Objectives:**

- Organisations must establish measurable AI objectives at relevant functions and levels.

- These objectives should be consistent with the AI policy and consider applicable requirements.

This comprehensive planning approach ensures that organisations proactively identify and address AI-related risks and opportunities while setting clear objectives for their AI initiatives.

6. Support

The standard outlines requirements for supporting the AI management system, including:

- Providing necessary resources for establishing, implementing, maintaining, and improving the AI management system.

- Ensuring competence of personnel involved in AI-related work.

- Promoting awareness of the AI policy and management system among staff.

- Establishing effective internal and external communication processes.

- Managing documented information related to the AI management system.

These support elements are crucial for the successful implementation and operation of the AI management system.

7. Operation

The operational aspects of the AI management system include:

- Operational planning and control to meet requirements and implement actions determined in the planning phase.

- Implementing controls related to the AI system development and usage lifecycle.

- Performing regular AI risk assessments and treatments.

- Conducting AI system impact assessments at planned intervals or when significant changes occur.

These operational requirements ensure that the AI management system is implemented and maintained throughout the organisation's AI-related activities.

8. Performance Evaluation

The standard requires organisations to evaluate the performance of their AI management system through:

- Monitoring, measurement, analysis, and evaluation of relevant aspects of the AI management system.

- Conducting internal audits at planned intervals to assess conformity and effectiveness.

- Management reviews to ensure the continuing suitability, adequacy, and effectiveness of the AI management system.

This performance evaluation process enables organisations to identify areas for improvement and ensure the ongoing effectiveness of their AI management system.

9. Improvement

The standard emphasises continual improvement of the AI management system, including:

- Addressing non-conformities and implementing corrective actions.

- Continually improving the AI management system's suitability, adequacy, and effectiveness.

This focus on improvement ensures that the AI management system remains relevant and effective in addressing evolving AI-related challenges and opportunities.

10. Annexes

The standard includes several annexes that provide additional guidance and resources:

- **Annex A (normative):** Reference control objectives and controls for AI management.

- **Annex B (normative):** Implementation guidance for AI controls.

- **Annex C (informative):** Potential AI-related organisational objectives and risk sources.

- **Annex D (informative):** Use of the AI management system across domains or sectors.

These annexes offer supplementary information to help organisations implement and maintain their AI management systems effectively.

Recommendations

Based on the analysis of AS ISO/IEC 42001:2023, the following recommendations are provided for organisations seeking to implement or improve their AI management systems:

1. Conduct a comprehensive assessment of the organisation's current AI-related activities, risks, and opportunities to establish a baseline for implementing the AI management system.

2. Develop a robust AI policy that aligns with the organisation's strategic objectives and addresses fundamental aspects of Responsible AI Development and Use.

3. Establish clear roles and responsibilities for AI management, ensuring top management involvement and commitment.

4. Implement a systematic AI risk assessment and treatment process, considering both technical and societal impacts of AI systems.

5. Develop and maintain documented procedures for key AI management processes, including risk assessment, impact assessment, and performance evaluation.

6. Provide adequate resources and training to ensure staff competence in AI management and awareness of the organisation's AI policy and objectives.

7. Regularly review and update the AI management system to ensure its effectiveness and alignment with evolving AI technologies and regulatory requirements.

8. Integrate the AI management system with existing organisational processes and management systems to ensure coherence and efficiency.

9. Implement a robust monitoring and measurement system to track the AI management system's performance and identify improvement areas.

10. Engage with relevant stakeholders, including customers, partners, and regulatory bodies, to ensure the AI management system addresses their needs and expectations.

Conclusion

The AS ISO/IEC 42001:2023 standard provides a comprehensive framework for organisations to establish, implement, maintain, and continually improve their Artificial Intelligence Management Systems. By adopting this standard, organisations can effectively address AI technologies' unique challenges and opportunities while ensuring responsible and ethical AI development and use.

The standard's emphasis on leadership commitment, risk management, and continual improvement aligns with best organisational management and governance practices. Its broad applicability across different types and sizes of organisations makes it a valuable tool for entities at various AI adoption and maturity stages.

Key strengths of the standard include its systematic approach to AI risk assessment and treatment, the requirement for regular impact assessments, and the focus on establishing clear AI policies and objectives. These elements enable organisations to proactively manage AI-related risks and opportunities, fostering trust among stakeholders and ensuring alignment with regulatory requirements.

Including normative annexes with reference controls and implementation guidance provides practical support for organisations implementing the standard. This guidance can be precious for organisations new to formalised AI management practices.

However, it's important to note that implementing an AI management system based on this standard requires significant commitment and resources. Organisations should be prepared to invest in developing new processes, training staff, and potentially restructuring existing operations to accommodate the standard's requirements.

In conclusion, AS ISO/IEC 42001:2023 offers a robust framework for organisations to manage their AI-related activities responsibly and effectively. By following the standard's requirements and recommendations, organisations can enhance their AI governance, mitigate risks, and capitalise on the opportunities presented by AI technologies.

As AI plays an increasingly important role in various industries, adopting this standard can provide a competitive advantage and demonstrate an organisation's commitment to responsible AI practices.

Further Reading

1. International Organization for Standardization (ISO) and International Electrotechnical Commission (IEC). "ISO/IEC 22989:2022 Information technology — Artificial intelligence — Artificial intelligence concepts and terminology." ISO, 2022.

2. International Organization for Standardization (ISO). "ISO/IEC 38507:2022 Information technology — Governance of IT — Governance implications of the use of artificial intelligence by organisations." ISO, 2022.

3. Dignum, Virginia. "Responsible Artificial Intelligence: How to Develop and Use AI in a Responsible Way." Springer Nature, 2019.

4. Artificial Intelligence Standards Hub. "AI Standards Hub." Available at: https://www.ai-standards.org/

5. World Economic Forum. "AI Governance: A Holistic Approach to Implement Ethics into AI." WEF, 2019.

ELEVEN

Other Relevant Frameworks and Legislation

While not exclusively focused on AI, several other frameworks and laws play crucial roles in governing AI use:

Cybercrime Act: This act comprehensively regulates computer and Internet-related offenses, such as unlawful access and computer trespass, damaging data and impeding access to computers, theft of data, computer fraud, cyberstalking harassment, and possession of child pornography.

The Cybercrime Act makes the following offences illegal (s.477.1 to s.478.4):

- Unauthorised access, modification, or impairment to commit a serious offence
- Unauthorised impairment of data to cause impairment
- Unauthorised impairment of electronic communications
- Possession of data with intent to commit a computer offence
- Supply of data with intent to commit a computer offence
- Unauthorised access to restricted data
- Unauthorised impairment of data held in a computer disk, credit card, etc.

Spam Act: This act established a scheme for regulating commercial email and other types of electronic messages. It restricts unauthorised, unsolicited electronic messages with some exceptions. This act is regulated by the "Australian Communications and Media Authority."

The full definition of Spam is "the sending of unsolicited commercial messages via email, SMS, MMS, and instant message either within Australia or to a device connected to an Australian service provider.

The three main rules of the Spam Act are:

- **Consent:** Only send commercial electronic messages with the addressee's consent, either express or inferred

- **Identification:** Include clear and accurate information about the person or business that is responsible for sending the commercial message

- **Unsubscribe:** Ensure that a functional unsubscribe facility is included in all commercial electronic messages and deal with unsubscribe requests promptly

Telecommunications (Interception and Access) Act: The primary objective of this act is to protect the privacy of individuals who use Australian telecommunication systems. Another purpose is to specify the circumstances under which it is lawful to intercede or access communications. This act covers both stored and real-time communications.

Security of Critical Infrastructure Act 2018: Imposes obligations relevant to AI systems in critical infrastructure. SOCI was expanded in 2024 to expand its oversight to eleven industrial sectors.

FEDERAL LAWS

1	Privacy Act 1988 (Cth)	• Governs the collection, use, disclosure, and handling of personal information.
		• Enforced through the Australian Privacy Principles (APPs).
		• Relevant for AI systems processing personal data.

FEDERAL LAWS

2	Australian Consumer Law (ACL)	• Part of the Competition and Consumer Act 2010 (Cth). • Protects consumers against unfair practices. • Applies to AI products and services, ensuring they are safe and fit for purpose.
3	Competition and Consumer Act 2010 (Cth)	• Regulates anti-competitive conduct. • Applicable if AI affects market competition or engages in misleading practices
4	Copyright Act (Cth)	• Protects intellectual property rights. • Relevant for AI-generated content and the use of copyrighted material in training AI models.
5	Criminal Code Act 1995 (Cth)	• Addresses cybercrime, including unauthorized access and data breaches. • Relevant for AI systems that could be exploited for criminal activities.
6	Defence and Strategic Goods List (DSGL) Customs Act 1901 (Cth)	• Controls the export of sensitive AI technologies.

FEDERAL LAWS

7	Anti-Money Laundering and Counter-Terrorism Financing Act 2006 (Cth)	• AI systems used in financial services must comply with financial regulations.
8	Foreign Influence Transparency Scheme Act 2018 (Cth)	• AI activities involving foreign entities may require registration and disclosure.
9	National Security Legislation Amendment (Espionage and Foreign Interference) Act 2018 (Cth)	• Relevant for AI systems that could impact national security.
10	Biosecurity Act 2015 (Cth)	• Relevant if AI is used in biosecurity applications.
11	Australian Prudential Regulation Authority (APRA) Standards	• For AI used in banking, insurance, and superannuation.
12	Australian Securities and Investments Commission (ASIC) Regulations	• AI in financial services must comply with ASIC's regulatory framework.
13	Broadcasting Services Act 1992 (Cth)	• AI used in media and broadcasting must adhere to content regulations.

DISCRIMINATION LAWS

14	Racial Discrimination Act 1975 (Cth)	• While many of the AI Standards and regulations emerging around the world specifically address discrimination of and by AI in many forms, there are existing laws that apply and require that AI systems must not discriminate based on protected attributes.
15	Sex Discrimination Act 1984 (Cth)	
16	Disability Discrimination Act 1992 (Cth)	• E.g.: the EU AI Act and several US States have laws about the use of AI in recruitment and the use of facial recognition AI.
17	Age Discrimination Act 2004 (Cth)	
18	Australian Human Rights Commission Act 1986 (Cth)	• Promotes human rights in Australia. • AI should align with human rights principles.
19	Defamation Laws	• Governed by both federal and state laws. • Applicable if AI disseminates defamatory content.

TELECOMS AND CYBERSECURITY LAWS

20	Telecommunications Act 1997 (Cth)	• Regulates telecommunications services. • Relevant for AI systems in communication networks.
21	Telecommunications Legislation Amendment (International Production Orders) Act 2020	• The Act enables Australia to enter into agreements with countries like the United States under the U.S. CLOUD Act framework.
22	Security of Critical Infrastructure Act 2018 (Cth)	• AI systems must comply with cybersecurity requirements, especially in critical infrastructure.
23	Telecommunications and Other Legislation Amendment Act 2017 (Cth)	
24	Surveillance Devices Act 2004 (Cth)	• Regulates the use of surveillance devices. • Relevant for AI systems involving monitoring or surveillance.

WORKPLACE HEALTH AND SAFETY, ENVIRONMENTAL LAWS

25	Work Health and Safety Act 2011 (Cth)	• AI systems in workplaces must ensure safety and compliance.
26	Therapeutic Goods Act 1989 (Cth)	• AI used in medical devices must comply with regulations for safety and efficacy.
27	Environment Protection and Biodiversity Conservation Act 1999 (Cth)	• AI applications affecting the environment must comply with environmental regulations

STATE AND TERRITORY LAWS

28	State Privacy Laws	• For example, Privacy and Data Protection Act 2014 (VIC), Privacy and Personal Information Protection Act 1998 (NSW)
29	State Anti-Discrimination Laws	• Vary by state, regulate the use of surveillance technologies, e.g.: Charter of Human Rights and Responsibilities Act 2006 (Victoria)
30	Surveillance and Listening Devices Acts	• Vary by state, regulate the use of surveillance technologies.

INTERNATIONAL AGREEMENTS AND TREATIES

31	OECD Principles on Artificial Intelligence	• Australia, as an OECD member, has adopted these principles promoting responsible stewardship of trustworthy AI
32	Universal Declaration of Human Rights (UDHR)	• AI use must respect human rights as outlined in the UDHR.
33	International Covenant on Civil and Political Rights (ICCPR)	• Australia is a signatory; AI applications should uphold civil and political rights.
34	Berne Convention for the Protection of Literary and Artistic Works	• Administered by WIPO; impacts AI in terms of international copyright laws.
35	Wassenaar Arrangement	• Controls the export of dual-use goods and technologies, including certain AI technologies.
36	APEC Cross-Border Privacy Rules (CBPR) System	• Facilitates data protection and privacy across APEC economies, relevant for AI handling personal data internationally
37	Trans-Pacific Partnership (TPP-11)	• Includes provisions on digital trade and data flows that may affect AI.
38	UNESCO Recommendation on the Ethics of Artificial Intelligence	• Australia participates in UNESCO initiatives promoting ethical AI use.

INTERNATIONAL AGREEMENTS AND TREATIES

39	Global Partnership on Artificial Intelligence (GPAI) (2020)	• Launched in June 2020, GPAI is an international initiative to support the responsible development and use of AI. • It facilitates collaboration between experts from industry, government, civil society, and academia.
40	G7 Leaders' Statements and the Hiroshima AI Process (2023)	• Advocates for the development of international standards through organizations like the International Organization for Standardization (ISO).
41	Council of Europe Framework Convention on Artificial Intelligence and Human Rights, Democracy and the Rule of Law (AI Convention)	• **Establish Common Standards:** Develop legally binding obligations for the design, development, and application of AI systems. • **Protect Fundamental Rights:** Ensure AI technologies respect human rights, democratic principles, and legal norms.
42	European Union's General Data Protection Regulation (GDPR)	• While not Australian law, affects Australian entities dealing with EU residents' data.

STANDARDS AND GUIDELINES

43	Australian AI Ethics Framework	• Developed by the Department of Industry, Science, Energy and Resources. • Provides voluntary principles for ethical AI development and use.
44	Standards Australia	• ISO/IEC 27001: Information Security Management. • ISO/IEC 27701: Privacy Information Management. • ISO/IEC 23894: AI Risk Management.
45	Australian Cyber Security Centre (ACSC) Information Security Manual (ISM)	• Provides guidelines for securing systems, including those involving AI.
46	CSIRO's Data61 Initiatives	• Publishes reports and guidelines on AI ethics and safety.
47	IEEE Global Initiative on Ethics of Autonomous and Intelligent Systems	• International standards influencing ethical AI practices in Australia.
48	National Transport Commission Guidelines	• For automated vehicles and AI in transportation.
49	Medical Board of Australia Guidelines	• Medical Board of Australia Guidelines.

STANDARDS AND GUIDELINES

50	Australian Competition and Consumer Commission (ACCC) Guidelines	• For digital platforms and consumer protection involving AI.
51	Banking Code of Practice	• AI in banking services must align with industry standards.
52	Telecommunications Consumer Protections Code	• For AI applications in telecommunications.
53	Safe Work Australia Codes of Practice	• AI systems must ensure workplace safety.

EMERGING REGULATIONS AND INITIATIVES

54	Australian Human Rights Commission's AI Guidelines	• Ongoing work to develop guidelines for human rights and AI.
55	National AI Action Plan	• Government initiatives to support responsible AI development.
56	Regulatory Sandboxes	• Facilitated by ASIC and APRA for innovation in fintech and AI.
57	Data Sharing and Release Legislation	• Proposed laws to govern sharing of government data involving AI.

Navigating the AI Governance Landscape

As we've explored throughout this book, the governance of artificial intelligence in Australia presents both significant challenges and immense opportunities. The rapid advancement of AI technologies offers the potential to drive innovation, enhance productivity, and improve the quality of life for Australians. However, it also brings risks that must be carefully managed to ensure that AI development and deployment align with ethical principles and societal values.

Australia has taken important steps towards establishing a robust framework for AI governance. The AI Ethics Principles, the Voluntary AI Safety Standard, and the Policy for the Responsible Use of AI in Government provide a strong foundation for responsible AI practices. These initiatives demonstrate Australia's commitment to being at the forefront of ethical AI development and use.

However, as we've seen, implementing these principles and standards is far from straightforward. The complexity of AI systems, the rapid pace of technological change, and the multifaceted nature of potential risks require a sophisticated, nuanced approach to governance. Organisations must navigate a landscape that includes technical, ethical, legal, and societal considerations, often with limited precedent to guide their decisions.

Key takeaways from this book include:

1. The critical importance of education and building AI literacy across all levels of an organisation.

2. The need for a measured, iterative approach to AI implementation, following the Plan-Do-Check-Adjust cycle.

3. The value of a comprehensive risk management framework tailored specifically to AI projects.

4. The necessity of ongoing stakeholder engagement and transparent communication about AI use and impacts.

5. The importance of staying adaptable in evolving technologies and regulatory environments.

While these principles provide a roadmap, the reality is that implementing effective AI governance is a complex, ongoing process that requires deep expertise and experience. Many organisations find themselves overwhelmed by the challenge of translating these principles into practical, day-to-day operations.

This is where expert guidance becomes invaluable. As one of Australia's leading authorities on AI governance, I have worked with organisations across various sectors to navigate these challenges successfully. My experience spans the development of AI strategies, implementation of governance frameworks, risk management, and stakeholder engagement.

If you need more certainty about how to proceed with AI governance in your organisation, I am here to help. The stakes are high, and the landscape is complex. But you don't have to navigate this terrain on your own.

I invite you to reach out for a consultation. Together, we can assess your organisation's specific needs, challenges, and opportunities in the AI space. We can develop a tailored strategy that aligns with best practices, regulatory requirements, and your business objectives.

Don't leave your AI governance to chance. Today's decisions will shape your organisation's future in the AI-driven world. Let's work together to ensure that your approach to AI is not just compliant but truly exemplary.

Contact me today to start your journey towards responsible, effective AI governance. Your organisation—and the Australians you serve—deserve nothing less than the best when it comes to managing the transformative power of AI.

Remember, in the rapidly evolving world of AI, staying ahead isn't just an advantage—it's a necessity. Let's build a future where your organisation leads the way in responsible AI use, setting new standards for innovation, ethics, and success.

Dr Darryl J Carlton has spent his entire adult life in information technology, almost 50 years. And while he keeps dreaming about one day getting a real job, frankly, this is all he knows, and as it turns out, he is quite good at it. He has found a niche, which he refers to as *"translating between business and technology"*. While his very first degree in 1983 was in Artificial Intelligence and expert systems, he has specialized in project management. He has run more than 30 projects with a combined value in excess of $3 Billion. He is committed to life-long learning. This is reflected in the fact that he is working towards a second Ph.D. He loves being on, under, or near the water. He scuba dives and sails. Even his dog Simba is a water dog!

Get my books and more here:

https://linktr.ee/darrylcarlton

Disclaimer:

The information provided here is for general informational purposes only and is not intended as legal advice. It is recommended to consult with a qualified legal professional for specific advice regarding your situation. The application of laws and regulations can vary based on individual circumstances and the specifics of each case.